262

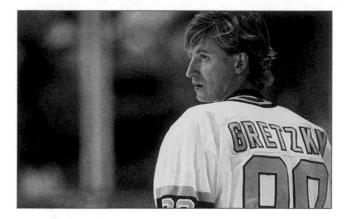

A NOTE TO PARENTS

When your children are ready to "step into reading," giving them the right books is as crucial as giving them the right food to eat. **Step into Reading Books** present exciting stories and information reinforced with lively, colorful illustrations that make learning to read fun, satisfying, and worthwhile. They are priced so that acquiring an entire library of them is affordable. And they are beginning readers with a difference—they're written on five levels.

Early Step into Reading Books are designed for brand-new readers, with large type and only one or two lines of very simple text per page. **Step 1 Books** feature the same easy-to-read type as the Early Step into Reading Books, but with more words per page. **Step 2 Books** are both longer and slightly more difficult, while **Step 3 Books** introduce readers to paragraphs and fully developed plot lines. **Step 4 Books** offer exciting nonfiction for the increasingly independent reader.

The grade levels assigned to the five steps—preschool through kindergarten for the Early Books, preschool through grade 1 for Step 1, grades 1 through 3 for Step 2, grades 2 through 3 for Step 3, and grades 2 through 4 for Step 4—are intended only as guides. Some children move through all five steps very rapidly; others climb the steps over a period of several years. Either way, these books will help your child "step into reading" in style!

Cover photo credits: Wayne Gretzky (Duomo/Al Tielemans); Gordie Howe (NHL Images/HHOF); Jacques Plante (Imperial Oil-Turofsky/Hockey Hall of Fame); Bobby Orr (*Sports Illustrated*/Neil Leifer); Bobby Hull (Bruce Bennett Studio Archives).

Text photo credits: page 1: Otto Greule/Allsport; page 7: *Sports Illustrated*/Tony Triolo; page 16: Imperial Oil-Turofsky/Hockey Hall of Fame; page 26: Bruce Bennett Studio Archives; page 30: National Hockey League; page 41: Ian Tomlinson/Allsport; page 44: Bruce Bennett Studio Archives.

www.randomhouse.com/kids

Library of Congress Cataloging-in-Publication Data
Kramer, Sydelle.
Hockey's greatest players / Sydelle Kramer. p. cm. — (Step into reading. A step 4 book) Summary: Introduces the origins and achievements of five talented and influential hockey players: Gordie Howe, Jacques Plante, Bobby Hull, Bobby Orr, and Wayne Gretzky. ISBN 0-679-88789-X (trade) — ISBN 0-679-98789-4 (lib. bdg.)
1. Hockey players—Biography—Juvenile literature. 2. Hockey players—Rating of—Juvenile literature. 3. National Hockey League—Juvenile literature. [1. Hockey players.] I. Title. II. Series: Step into reading. Step 4 book. GV848.5.A1K734 1999
796.962'092'2—dc21   [b]   98-48896

Printed in the United States of America 10 9 8 7 6 5 4 3 2 1
STEP INTO READING is a registered trademark of Random House, Inc.

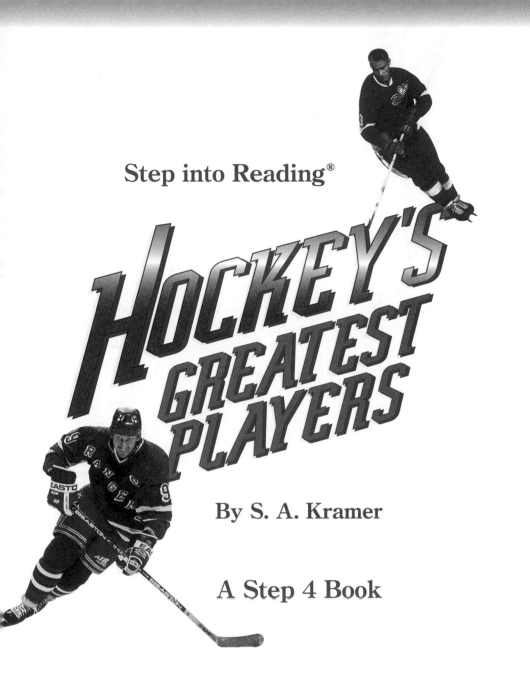

Step into Reading®

HOCKEY'S GREATEST PLAYERS

By S. A. Kramer

A Step 4 Book

Random House 🏠 New York

INTRODUCTION

Hard, cold ice. Skates with blades as sharp as knives. Long, curved sticks that whip through the air. A three-inch rubber puck moving as fast as a bullet. Players crashing into one another at top speed. Which sport has them all? The fastest, roughest, and most violent professional game—ice hockey.

A hockey rink can be a dangerous place. These days, no one dares skate unprotected. Athletes cover and pad almost every inch of their bodies. They have to. In each game, they're tripped, elbowed, hooked, slashed, high-sticked, and slammed against the boards. Pucks bang into them at over 100 miles per hour.

Ice hockey originated in Canada in the 1850s. The puck that was used then was square, not round. Hockey quickly became a Canadian favorite.

The United States didn't discover hockey until the 1890s. Even after the National Hockey League was founded in 1917, few Americans followed the game. And fewer played it. It wasn't until the 1990s that ice hockey became a prime-time American sport.

Today's NHL clubs have a truly international roster. Players come from *everywhere*—Russia, Scandinavia, and Eastern Europe, as well as Canada and the United States. Facing off on a rink 200 feet long and 85 feet wide, teams have just one thing in mind—putting the puck into the net.

Over the years, a handful of athletes have changed the way hockey is played. They're the game's greatest stars. And this book is all about them.

THE BRUISER

Gordie Howe skates hard down the ice. Like all other players of the day, he's not wearing a helmet. Knees bent, body leaning forward, he heads straight for the man with the puck. Gordie is the game's roughest checker. He's determined to keep the man from scoring.

It's March 28, 1950. Gordie's Detroit Red Wings are in the second period of a playoff game against the Toronto Maple Leafs. Detroit is behind, 3-0. One more Maple Leaf goal, and the Red Wings will surely be finished. They're counting on Gordie to keep them in the game.

A star right wing, Gordie is famous for his fighting. He's gentle off the ice, but brutal on it. Big, strong, and tireless, he'll use his elbow or his stick to knock a man flat.

Now Gordie's long stride and powerful legs take him down the rink in a flash. With his stick up, he hurls himself at his opponent. He plans to bash the man against the boards.

The plan doesn't work. The Toronto player sees him coming. He quickly passes the puck and tries to get out of the way. But Gordie can't stop. He brushes past the player, trips, and smashes his face into the boards.

Silent and still, he lies on the ice. A river of

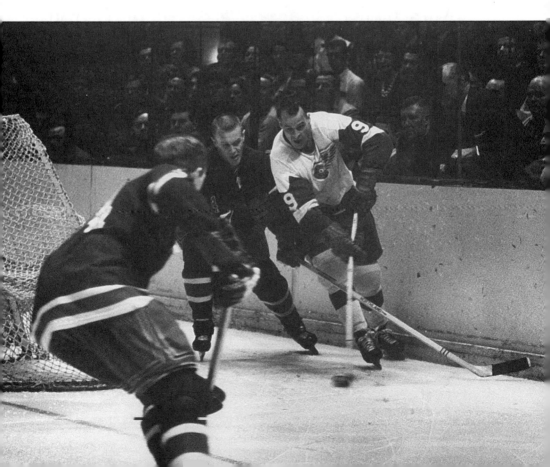

blood flows from his forehead, nose, and cheek. Soon all the ice around him is red.

A stretcher carries the unconscious Gordie off the ice. An ambulance rushes him to the hospital. Doctors discover he has a broken nose and cheekbone and a cut eyeball. But worst of all, he's smashed his skull. His brain is bleeding.

Gordie needs immediate surgery. For two days, no one knows if he will live or die.

Miraculously, he recovers. All of Detroit celebrates. Fans send him get-well cards and gifts. The Red Wings, inspired, win the play-offs and then the Stanley Cup.

Gordie's in the arena for the final victory. When the fans spot him, they chant, "We want Howe!" Wearing a hat to cover his injured head, Gordie walks out on the ice. The crowd goes wild over its hero.

His brush with death makes Gordie even tougher. He's back with the Red Wings the next season—and doesn't miss a single game.

Gordie goes on to a true superstar career. Between 1950 and 1968, he misses only twenty games. For twenty seasons in a row, he's among the NHL's top five scorers. With him on their side, Detroit wins seven league championships and four Stanley Cups.

Yet no one ever expected Gordie to be a success. His father once said, "I never thought he'd amount to anything." Fans doubted him, too. After all, he scored only seven goals in his rookie year.

One of nine children, Gordie grew up in Saskatchewan, Canada. His family was poor. Porridge was sometimes the only food they had. As a young boy, Gordie was sickly and clumsy. He was so shy that he wouldn't go into a store alone to buy an ice cream.

School made him miserable. He failed third grade twice. His classmates called him

"Doughhead," local slang for "stupid."

Hockey was his escape. Gordie got his first pair of skates when he was five and a half. They were so big that he had to wear five pairs of socks to fill them. His family couldn't afford to buy him equipment, so he never used pads or gloves. Instead of a puck, he'd whack tennis balls or chunks of ice.

Nothing could take him away from hockey. He'd be on the ice even when it was fifty below zero outside. For practice, he'd skate to school and back on the frozen roads. "On the weekends," Gordie said, "I never took the skates off." He even ate with them on.

His talent was amazing. It made him feel more confident. Then when he was fifteen, a Red Wings' scout saw him playing in a junior league. He was skating for the Red Wings by the age of eighteen. In his very first game, he scored a goal—and lost two teeth.

But during his rookie season, Gordie

brawled more than he scored. It was as though he had to prove he couldn't be pushed around. The next year he concentrated on getting the puck into the net, becoming one of the most accurate shooters ever.

Some fans were surprised that Gordie scored so easily. He never looked as if he was skating that quickly. On the ice, his head bobbed up and down and he blinked constantly.

But his lightning reflexes enabled him to outrace everyone to the puck. Using his long arms and huge hands, he blasted his wrist shot at 114 miles per hour. A master stick-handler, he could score left- or right-handed.

Whether on offense or defense, Gordie never stopped fighting. If someone hit him, he always struck back. Players were afraid of him and his ferocious style of hockey. One said, "He is…the most vicious, cruel, and mean man I've ever met in a hockey game."

Outside the rink, though, Gordie was different. With his sad brown eyes, he was often bashful, mumbling his words. Hating arguments, he went out of his way to avoid them. He answered every fan letter personally, so delighted was he to be a star.

By the end of his NHL career, Gordie was scarred and bruised. He had over 300 stitches in his face and had lost twelve teeth. He'd also spent thirty *hours* in the penalty box!

No one had ever appeared in more NHL games. But after he retired, Gordie found that he missed the sport terribly. So he made a comeback in another league (the WHA, or World Hockey Association—now defunct), skating on a team with two of his sons. He didn't stop playing until he was fifty-two!

Gordie was a legend. Despite the violence of his game, athletes like Wayne Gretzky modeled themselves after him. As one player said, "Whichever way the puck bounced, he'd play it right."

GORDON (GORDIE) HOWE
(Big Fellow, Blinky, Power)
6', 205 lbs.

Born: March 31, 1928

Position: Right wing

Career: 1946–80

Played for the Detroit Red Wings, the Houston Aeros, and the Hartford Whalers.

Hall of Fame

Feats:

1. Most NHL seasons played (26).
2. Most NHL games played (1,767).
3. Most goals by a right wing (801).
4. Most assists by a right wing (1,049).
5. Second in total points (1,850).
6. Second in total goals (801).
7. Second in total assists (1,049).
8. Named MVP six times.
9. Named an All-Star 21 times.
10. Led the NHL in scoring six times.

Greatest Feat:

From 1950–69, he finished in the top five in NHL scoring each year.

THE MASK

New York City. November 1, 1959. It's the first period of a game between the Montreal Canadiens and the New York Rangers. Thirty-year-old Jacques Plante is the Canadiens' star goalie. As he guards the net, fans can see his serious face. Like all goalies of the time, he doesn't wear a mask or a helmet.

With no protection, Jacques has had many injuries. In just six NHL seasons, his face has needed over 200 stitches. His nose has been broken four times, his cheekbones twice, and his jaw once.

Now he crouches in the net. When a swarm of players crowds the crease, all he can see are flying bodies and flapping arms and legs. He's got to block the puck—but where is it?

Fifteen feet away, the Ranger player fires. All at once Jacques spots a rising black bullet speeding toward him. It's zeroing in at 100 miles per hour. He can't get out of its way.

Bam! The puck smashes into Jacques's left nostril. He topples to the ice.

The game is stopped. Jacques's teammates help him off the ice. In the training room, he gets seven stitches to close the three-inch gash. He wants to go back to the rink—but this time with his face shielded.

A while before, Jacques had a special piece of equipment made for him. It's a white fiberglass mask. So far he's worn it only in practice. The mask has two slits for his eyes and a hole for his mouth. It's only an eighth of an inch thick, but pucks just glance off it.

Jacques has never been allowed to wear the mask in games. His coach believes the mask will interfere with his sight.

Jacques disagrees. He's sure he'll play better with the mask. Free from worry about

getting hurt, he'll be able to block the puck more effectively. Tonight's injury is the last straw. From the first-aid table, he tells the coach, "I won't go back without the mask."

Jacques takes the mask out of his equipment bag and straps it over his bandaged face. As he skates onto the ice, the crowd cheers, then falls silent. To them, Jacques looks like a witch doctor, not a hockey player. One man shouts out, "Hey, Plante, take that thing off! Halloween's over."

Jacques doesn't listen. Stopping shot after shot, he helps the Canadiens win, 3-1. The team goes on to take ten games in a row. Jacques has proved that the mask works.

But some players think he's a coward. One reporter calls him the "Faceless Wonder." Jacques doesn't care. With his mask, he wins his fifth consecutive Vezina Trophy for best goaltender in the NHL. And the Canadiens take their fifth Stanley Cup in a row.

Soon, other NHL goalies begin to wear masks. They wouldn't have been able to if Jacques hadn't made a stand. He was always a person who thought for himself. One team-mate said, "He *had* to be different."

Born in Quebec, Canada, Jacques was the oldest of eleven children. His family had so little money, they could afford soda only at Christmas. Jacques had to help his mother clean, cook, and do laundry. He even had to learn how to knit.

Jacques started playing hockey when he was just three. Like Gordie Howe, he used a tennis ball for a puck. He made his pads out of boards and potato sacks. By the time he was twelve, he was a goalie. At fifteen, he was playing for the local factory's team. He earned fifty cents a game.

After graduating from high school, Jacques went to the minor leagues. Then in 1952, he joined the Canadiens. His great goal-tending helped make the club a winner.

Yet no matter how many shots he blocked, Jacques never stopped thinking about how to improve. He was the first goalie to leave the cage to chase down a loose puck. Armed with a great memory, he knew by heart where opponents liked to put their shots. He even kept a written record of each player's strengths and weaknesses.

Jacques's talent made him great. But it

didn't make him popular. Many of his team-mates found him moody and distant. They disliked and even distrusted him.

If Jacques threw his arms in the air after a victory, his teammates thought he was trying to hog the credit. When asthma made him sick, they felt he was imagining it. After he played poorly in the 1960–61 season, they didn't believe him when he said he'd hurt his knee.

Sent to the minors, Jacques came roaring back to the NHL after a knee operation. The next year he played in every game and again won the Vezina Trophy. He was also named the league's MVP (Most Valuable Player).

By the time he retired, 30,000 shots had been fired at him. Hc'd also won the Vezina a record seven times. "The mask did it," he said.

Even after he left the rink, the mask stayed part of his life. In 1970, he started his own business—making hockey masks!

JOSEPH JACQUES OMER PLANTE
(Jake the Snake)
6', 175 lbs.

Born: January 17, 1929

Position: Goalie

Career: 1952–75

Played for the Montreal Canadiens, the New York Rangers, the St. Louis Blues, the Toronto Maple Leafs, the Boston Bruins, and the Edmonton Oilers.

Hall of Fame

Feats:

1. Second in games won (434).
2. Second in playoff shutouts (15).
3. Fourth in total shutouts (82).
4. Fifth in playoff wins (71).
5. Named MVP in 1962 (one of only four goaltenders to be so honored).
6. Was the first goalie ever to win the Vezina Trophy five years in a row.

Greatest Feat:

Seven Vezina Trophies, the most ever.

SLAP SHOT

Ontario, Canada. December 25, 1942. Little Bobby Hull races down the stairs. There's a special present from his dad under the Christmas tree.

Bobby rips the gift open. Ice skates! It's his first pair, and he can't wait to try them out. When his mother says, "Remember…no crying or the skates go back to Santa," Bobby just smiles. He knows he's going to have a great time.

Fifty yards from the house, the bay is frozen over. Bobby's two older sisters take him onto the ice. Within a couple of hours, he's skating without their help. He loves it so much that it's nearly dark before he finally comes inside.

Bobby's father is pleased. He wants Bobby to play hockey. He was once a terrific player himself, but he had to give the sport up to support his family. Now he'd like Bobby to do what he couldn't—become a star.

Bobby's only four, but his dad teaches him to play hockey. By the time he's five, he's out-playing kids twice his age. Every morning at dawn, he's on the ice. He practices again after school, then again after dinner. Bobby says, "Mum would have to send my sisters out to bring me home to bed."

By the time he's ten, Bobby's in four different junior hockey leagues. Sometimes he scores twenty-five goals a day. At twelve he's so good, he's skating against adults. A scout for the Chicago Blackhawks has his eye on him.

Bobby's father is proud. But he wants his son to do even better. Somehow he's convinced Bobby isn't trying hard enough.

While Bobby's mother compliments him after games, his dad asks why he doesn't score more. At times, Bobby feels there's no way he can please his father. But he keeps trying.

More than anything, Bobby's dad wants him to play in the NHL. It's Bobby's dream, too. To make it, however, Bobby needs better coaching than he can get at home. So when he's only fourteen, he moves to a new city and lives with another family.

His mother visits him every weekend, but being away is hard. Bobby gets into trouble in school. He doesn't follow his coach's orders. Yet he's so skillful in the rink that the NHL wants him. By the age of eighteen, Bobby has quit high school and joined the Blackhawks.

A rookie left wing in 1957, Bobby feels nervous and insecure. But the more he plays, the more relaxed he becomes. Two seasons later, when he's just twenty-one, he becomes the second youngest player ever to win the scoring title.

Skating without a helmet, Bobby's a blond blur in the rink. Reaching speeds close to thirty miles per hour, he's easily the fastest man on the ice. Fans and teammates call him the Golden Jet.

A graceful skater, Bobby never seems to get tired. Big and strong, he can slow down, then speed up easily. Shooting left-handed, he uses a heavy stick with a slight bend and curved blade. He feels it gives him better control of the puck.

Bobby's muscular arms, chest, and back make him the most powerful shooter ever. His aim is deadly, even from sixty feet out. Reaching back with his stick, he blasts his slap shot 118.3 miles per hour!

Goalies trying to block Bobby's shot often get knocked down by the force of the puck. It slams in so hard that it sometimes tears their glove off. One goalie who got hit said, "It felt like I had been seared by a branding iron."

With such a great shot, Bobby's a scoring machine. He's the first man to get more than fifty goals in one season. Over the years, he wins three scoring titles. He makes putting the puck in the net look easy.

Defenders try to double-team, or even triple-team, him. They grab his arm, jump on his back, and check him hard. But Bobby just scoots back around his net and charges down the ice, stickhandling with one hand and pushing off opponents with the other.

He pays a high price for his scoring success. Often injured, he gets huge scars on his face. After just a few NHL seasons, all his front teeth are missing. His nose is broken so many times, it ends up bent sideways on his face.

Yet Bobby keeps on skating no matter how hard he's clobbered. In his first eight

seasons, he misses only eight games. Even more remarkable, he always plays the game cleanly. He might be hooked, slashed, or elbowed, but he rarely loses his temper.

Some players think he's *too* nice and ought to start hitting back. But Bobby knows that his job is to score, not fight. Because of him, the Blackhawks win the 1961 Stanley Cup. It's their first championship in twenty-three years.

Experts as well as fans feel Bobby's the most exciting hockey player of his time. He's also the most popular. Wherever he skates, crowds applaud his goals. Always signing autographs, he seems to have a smile for everyone. Even his opponents admire him.

But Bobby never feels satisfied with his game. It's as if he believes what his father said long ago—he ought to score more goals. After each game, he stays behind and smacks pucks at the practice goalie. His coach says, "He spends more time shooting in practices than any player on the team."

In 1972, Bobby quits the NHL, joining the WHA to earn more money. By the time he retires, he's hockey's greatest left wing ever. More important, he's proved all his father's doubts wrong. He's proud that he's passed his talent on to his son, Brett Hull of the Dallas Stars. Being a scoring and skating champion runs in the family.

ROBERT (BOBBY) MARVIN HULL
(Golden Jet, Golden Boy)
5'10", 193 lbs.

Born: January 3, 1939

Position: Left wing

Career: 1957–80

Played for the Chicago Blackhawks, the Winnipeg Jets
  (as player and player-coach), and the Hartford Whalers.

Hall of Fame

Feats:

1. Led the NHL in goals seven times (more seasons
   than any other player).
2. Most goals by a left wing (610).
3. Sixth in total goals (610).
4. First player to score more than 50 goals in a season
   (54 in 1965–66).
5. Led the NHL in scoring three times.
6. Named MVP two times.
7. Won the Lady Byng Trophy for gentlemanly play
   (1964–65).

Greatest Feat:

In 1964–65, Bobby was named MVP, dominating the game yet
spending only 32 minutes in the penalty box. Who says nice
guys finish last?

DEFENSE!

Boston, Massachusetts. May 10, 1970. It's the fourth game of the best-of-seven Stanley Cup finals between the Boston Bruins and the St. Louis Blues. The Bruins haven't won the Cup since 1941. Everyone's counting on Bobby Orr to change the team's luck.

Bobby is Boston's star defenseman—but he's also a top scorer. The first defenseman to also play great offense, he has single-handedly changed hockey forever. Always on the attack, he's still the first man back to defend. He's the Bruins' leader, blocking the puck at one end of the ice and putting it into the net at the other.

He and his Bruins lead the Cup series, 3–0. They want to win the championship tonight, in front of the home crowd. But the Blues won't give in. They push the game into overtime with a 3–3 tie. Now sudden death will decide the victor.

Bobby hears the shouts of the 14,835 fans. He knows they're waiting for him to make his move. Just after overtime begins, he sees the puck get loose in the St. Louis end. This is his chance to end the game fast.

Like lightning, Bobby outskates the Blues to the puck. Spotting a teammate in the corner, he slaps a long pass to him. Then Bobby breaks toward the net forty feet away. It takes him only three strides to hit full speed.

The teammate passes the puck back to Bobby. As usual, Bobby has no trouble controlling it. A defender tries to whack him, but he's nearly impossible to knock down. He zooms in on the goalie and fires off a shot.

The puck looks on target, but Bobby trips on the goalie's stick. He flies ten feet through the air and crashes flat. Sprawled on the ice, he doesn't know where the puck is.

The red light flashes over the net. The puck has slid between the goalie's legs! Bobby's scored! Just forty seconds into overtime, he's won the game.

Boston has swept the series. The fans stand and cheer. His teammates swarm together and carry Bobby around the rink.

From the top of the arena, crepe paper floats down, staining the ice orange, yellow, and blue. Kids race onto the rink, waving colored streamers. When they snatch the Bruins' sticks, no one seems to care. Everyone's beaming. Bobby says, "It's the happiest moment of my life."

Experts agree it's the perfect end to one of the greatest seasons a hockey player has ever had. Just twenty-two years old, Bobby wins the scoring title and is named MVP, playoff MVP, and the year's best defenseman. He's the only man to ever win four individual awards in one year. His coach says Bobby "may be the greatest athlete who ever lived."

Yet when he was a child in Parry Sound, Ontario, Bobby was too small for the game. At the age of twelve he was only five foot two, and his hockey shirt hung down to his knees. Though he'd been skating in a league since he was five, few people believed any team would want someone so short and thin.

But Bobby was stronger than he looked. He could outrace any player. With his quick feet and strong legs, he wove through every defense. He could steal the puck and score easily with his hard, low shot.

By fourteen, he was growing and playing junior hockey against adults. At sixteen, he was a star, setting junior scoring records for defensemen. By the time he was eighteen, he was famous throughout Canada. He quit high school and joined the Bruins. Close to his family, he cried when he left home.

Boston fans expected great things from Bobby from the start. Even in his rookie season of 1966–67, huge crowds turned out to see him. They weren't disappointed. His first goal was a hard shot from forty-five feet out. The fans gave him a three-minute standing ovation.

But he didn't rest on his laurels. He was

tough on himself. Once, he made a mistake, went to the bench, and cried. Despite the fans' praise, he stayed modest. That first season, he was so shy that he called each of his teammates "sir."

The very next year, Bobby became the heart and soul of the Bruins. His teammates counted on him to take the puck and invent new plays. Completely unpredictable on the ice, he never made the same move twice.

On defense, Bobby killed power plays by skating in circles with the puck. He'd throw his body around fearlessly to stop opponents. One player said being checked by Bobby "was like getting hit by a pickup truck."

On offense, his most famous move was a spin like a dancer's. With defensemen around him, he'd suddenly twirl. The trick fooled them into skating right by him. Unguarded, he'd take the puck to the net.

Bobby was such a star, even people who

didn't know much about hockey admired him. Fans tracked him down at home to get his autograph. To protect his privacy, he had to move every year and keep his address secret!

With Bobby on their side, the Bruins won two Stanley Cups. For eight years in a row, he was named the NHL's best defenseman. He may have been a superstar, but he always acted like one of the guys. When he was on the bench, he'd cheer his teammates on.

"Hockey is my life," he said. He practiced hard. Arriving early for each game, he'd drink a lot of orange juice for energy. Before the team took the ice, he'd lift his stick like a magic wand. Touching the pads of his teammates, he'd wish them all luck.

Boston was a rough, tough club, and Bobby was a scrapper. While he never slashed with his stick, he was known to throw a punch. He was unafraid of getting hurt. When a puck shot through the air, he'd use any part of his body to block it.

But his bruising style of hockey left him battered. By the age of thirty, he'd had ten operations on his left knee alone. Although he was still a young man, he could no longer skate. He had no choice but to retire after only twelve seasons.

Bobby's career may have been short, but he left his mark on hockey. He was the first player in the game to be world-famous. Before most athletes did, he hired an agent, showing other stars how to make sure they were paid well.

Despite his wealth, he was never flashy. A generous man, he gave large sums of money to charity. He often visited children in hospitals and orphanages. A star on the ice, he was a hero off it as well.

ROBERT GORDON (BOBBY) ORR
6', 199 lbs.

Born: March 20, 1948

Position: Defenseman

Career: 1966–78

Played for the Boston Bruins and the Chicago Blackhawks.
Hall of Fame

Feats:

1. Won the Norris Trophy as the NHL's best defenseman eight years in a row (1968–75).
2. Best career scoring average for a defenseman (fifth overall).
3. Named MVP three years in a row (1970–72).
4. Named playoff MVP twice (1970 and 1972).
5. Named Rookie of the Year (1966–67).
6. Was the only defenseman ever to be the NHL league's leading scorer. (He did it twice, in 1970 and 1975.)
7. First player ever to have more than 100 assists in a season (1970–71).
8. Most assists ever in a single season for a defenseman (102 in 1970–71).
9. Most assists in a season five times.
10. Most points in a season for a defenseman (139 in 1970–71).

Greatest Feat:

In 1970, Bobby had what some consider the greatest season ever by any hockey player. He became the only man ever to win four individual awards in one season (MVP, best defenseman, leading scorer, and playoff MVP). He was only 22 years old at the time.

HAT TRICK

New York City. April 23, 1997. The New York Rangers are struggling. The Florida Panthers are shutting them out, 1–0. It's the second period of Game Four in the first round of the Stanley Cup playoffs. The crowd in New York's Madison Square Garden is eager for a win. That will give the Rangers a commanding 3–1 lead in the seven-game series. All eyes are on Wayne Gretzky. Can the Rangers' center come through?

Not everyone thinks Wayne can deliver. He may be nicknamed the Great One and hold or share sixty-one NHL records, but some fans say the thirty-six-year-old superstar is past his prime. He's scored more goals, assists, and points than any player in history, but these days opponents seem to be knocking him around at will.

Wayne, though, knows he's not finished. He's heard people doubt his talent before. In 1979–80, his first NHL season, some experts said he'd never make it. They felt he wasn't strong enough, fast enough, or big enough for the pros. In the rink, he was reluctant to fight. He didn't even hit the puck that hard.

Wayne proved his doubters wrong. His shots found the net as though drawn by a magnet. Defenders couldn't keep up with him. He combined slippery moves with great balance to roll right off checks. Constantly on the go, he followed his own advice—"Find open ice." Somehow he always figured out where the puck was going next.

The fans in the Garden want to see if he still has the magic touch. The Rangers are on a power play. Can Wayne score? As he glides down the ice, there's a frown on his face. He doesn't like the way he's been playing.

Bent forward at the waist, he clutches his short, heavy stick. His skates are a size and a half too small for him, but that's the way he likes them. The right side of his jersey is tucked deep into his pants. Wayne believes he can't score if it comes out.

With total concentration, Wayne's busy coming up with a plan. Fans are surprised when he doesn't take the puck and head to his "office"—the area right behind the opponents' net. A terrific passer, he can see the whole rink from there and send the puck to the open man, or sneak it past the goalie.

Wayne realizes this game calls for something different. Always thinking, he skates to the right circle, on the goalie's left side. When a teammate passes the puck to him, he fires a wrist shot—goal! Now the game is tied.

The crowd is thrilled. But they have no idea what he'll do next. Neither do the Panthers. After all, Wayne's an athlete who can

pass with his skate as well as his stick. He's been known to score by flipping the puck off a goalie's back. One player says, "He has the greatest moves I've ever seen."

Sure enough, he creates another great play. Left-handed Wayne takes a cross-ice pass on the run. Somehow he always makes the most difficult moves look easy. Once again at the right circle, he bangs a slap shot over the goalie's left shoulder. It goes into the net!

The fans jump to their feet, cheering. Wayne raises his right arm high. The Rangers now lead, 2–1.

But he isn't through. He wants to put this game away. Less than three minutes later, Wayne controls the puck with his long reach. Racing down the right side, he suddenly stops, kicking up a spray of ice. Then, faking a shot, he fools the defenseman. Now he's wide open. It's just him and the goalie.

Wayne rips his stick through the air. It's another hard slap shot. The puck hits the left post—and angles in!

The crowd goes crazy. Fans toss hats and caps onto the ice. Wayne throws both arms in the air and heads for the bench.

Wayne's scored a hat trick. In just six minutes and twenty-three seconds, he's gotten *three* goals. Full of emotion, he says of his feat, "It's pretty special." The Rangers go on to win the game, 3–1, and then the series.

Three weeks later, Wayne does it again. He gets his tenth career playoff hat trick against the Philadelphia Flyers. Now he's scored a total of fifty-nine hat tricks, the most ever. The Rangers lose the series, but Wayne has triumphed. He's shown everyone age doesn't matter—he's *still* a superstar.

Most experts agree Wayne is the greatest player in hockey history. There's never been an athlete who understood the game the way he does.

Born in Brantford, Ontario, Wayne was skating at two. When he was four, his dad flooded the backyard to make him a rink. The cold winter air froze it completely. His grandmother, a big hockey fan, helped Wayne learn to shoot when he was five. He aimed shot after shot at her as she played goalie while sitting in a chair.

By the age of six, hockey was Wayne's life. He'd spend even more time practicing each week than he spent at school. Then, at ten, he scored 378 goals in just 85 games! Canadian TV broadcast a special about him. Shy, quiet

Wayne hated the attention.

His talent made him unpopular with his teammates' parents. As long as Wayne was on the ice, their children skated in his shadow. They decided not to let him join his home team for junior hockey. In order to play, he had to leave home at fourteen and join another city's club.

When Wayne was just sixteen, *Sports Illustrated* ran a story on him. At eighteen, he was in the NHL, becoming the only rookie to ever win the MVP. He was also the youngest player in history to make the All-Star team. This was only the beginning.

Wayne played as if he had eyes in the back of his head. He could see everything that was going on in the rink. The flow of the game was so clear to him, he said, "it's like everything is happening in slow motion."

A great team player, he helped the Edmonton Oilers win four Stanley Cups in five years. But he never let his success go to his head. Ever polite, Wayne didn't have temper tantrums. He refused to take his talent for granted, working hard to stay in shape. In his first fourteen seasons, he missed only thirty-nine games.

Like Bobby Hull, Wayne is a superstar who never played dirty. His success has shown kids they don't need to fight to win. He was never the most powerful guy in the rink—only the best.

WAYNE DOUGLAS GRETZKY
(The Great One, Gretz)
6', 170 lbs.

Born: January 26, 1961

Position: Center

Career: 1979–

Played for the Edmonton Oilers, the Los Angeles Kings, the St. Louis Blues, and the New York Rangers.

Feats:

1. Most total points (2,795).
2. Most total assists (1,910).
3. Most total goals (885).
4. Most 100-or-more-point seasons (14).
5. Most single-season goals (92 in 1981–82).
6. Most single-season assists (163 in 1985–86).
7. Most single-season points (215 in 1985–86).
8. Most total playoff goals, assists, and points.
9. Named MVP nine times, the most ever, including eight years in a row.
10. Won the scoring title ten times, including seven in a row.
11. Most assists in a season 14 times, including 13 in a row.
12. Once scored four goals in just one period (February 18, 1981).

Greatest Feat:

Scored at least one point in 51 games in a row—a record.

MORE GREATS

Howarth William (Howie) Morenz: The game's first superstar, he played in the NHL from 1923 to 1937. Known for his furious charge down center ice to score, he'd skate straight for an opponent and deliberately knock him down. He played the ukulele as he traveled between games.

Joseph Henri Maurice (Rocket) Richard: Playing for the Montreal Canadiens, Rocket terrified goalies between 1942 and 1960. He was the first player ever to score fifty goals in one season (1944–45). Strong, with a fiery temper, he was famous for fighting—not just with opponents but also with officials. His menacing dark eyes were described by one goalie as "lit up, flashing and gleaming like a pinball machine." He holds the record for most goals in a playoff game and most overtime goals.

Mario Lemieux: One of the greatest scorers in hockey history, he played for the Pittsburgh

Penguins from 1984 to 1997. A French Canadian, he barely spoke English when he joined the NHL. He learned the language from watching American TV. At the height of his career, he discovered a lump in his neck, which turned out to be cancerous. He recovered after treatment and returned to hockey, ending up winning six scoring titles. Injuries forced him to quit at thirty-one, but he still holds the record for goals per game average. He's sixth in total points and seventh in career goals.

Mark Messier: Known as the "bad boy" of hockey for his bruising checking style, Mess only has to stare at an opponent to scare him. A true leader, he expects victories, then makes sure they happen. Even as a child, he took control of bad situations. Given a horse that no one could tame, he broke, then rode him. In the top five in career points, he's second in playoff goals and points, and sixth in total assists.